Ready to Pray

A Spiritual Journey of Prayer and Worship

Gail E. Dudley

Cover Design

Becky Jacobsen
Photographer

Editing

Stephanie Bright-Mayberry
Bright Ideas Creative Design and Consulting

Copyediting and Interior Page Formatting

Kathy Curtis
klcur321@bellsouth.net
www.christianbookformat.com

Published by Gail E. Dudley
Highly Recommended International, Inc.
Ministry In Motion Ministries International
The Church at North Pointe
www.GetRealLife.net
Columbus, Ohio
United States of America
614-441-8178
e-mail: GED@MIMToday.org

PROCLAMATION

A cts 12:5, 16-17 speaks to us clearly and with great power that God will move as we pray for ourselves and intercede on behalf of others.

> *"⁵So Peter was kept in prison, but the church was earnestly praying to God for him. ¹⁶But Peter kept on knocking, and when they opened the door and saw him, they were astonished. ¹⁷Peter motioned with his hand for them to be quiet and described how the Lord had brought him out of prison."*

In the name of Jesus, I declare and decree your freedom in Jesus. I bow before the Father humbly submitting on your behalf that your prayer life will take you to a new level in Christ. I pray that when you kneel before the Father on behalf of others, they will be healed, forgiven, delivered, renewed, refreshed, and that many will ask, "What must I do to be saved?" May your prayer life take you deeper in Christ. I pray from this day forward that you step out on faith and live as God, our Father in heaven, has ordained for you to live.

In Obedience to Christ,

SPECIAL THANKS

My Heartfelt Appreciation to…

My husband, Kevin, whom I love and call "friend." You are truly a man after the heart of God. I will always be grateful to the Lord for allowing our paths to cross and for joining us as husband and wife. Please know that I pray for you at all times. Every time I see your face, smell your scent, hear your voice, or have your name dropped in my spirit from the Lord, I pray for you.

To my son and daughter, Alex and Dominiq, who encourage me and challenge me to press towards the prize — the high calling of Jesus. The two of you have my heart. Please know I pray for you daily.

A special thanks to Stephanie Bright-Mayberry who selflessly gave of her time and self to edit this book to completion. I praise God for your talent and for laboring with me on this project.

I am truly indebted to Kathy Curtis (www.christian bookformat.com) for preparing this book to go to another level in Christ, reaching the nations and preparing people to be *Ready to Pray*. She gave of herself and put aside other jobs to see this come to completion. The Lord has connected us in the Spirit and for that I say, "Thank you!"

Most importantly, my deepest gratitude to Jesus Christ, our Lord and Savior. Thank you, God, for Your grace and mercy and for Your truth and love, and to the Holy Spirit for His continued guidance in everything I do.

CONTENTS

Contents

FOREWORD

In order to teach about spiritual disciplines and come across as knowledgeable and believable, the teacher must first journey through the lessons she will teach. In *Ready to Pray*, Gail Dudley shares the life lessons that the Lord has poured into her life through her spiritual journey with Him. Whether these were seasons of joy, seasons of sorrow, seasons of want, or seasons of plenty, the Lord has been working in Gail's life for many years, teaching her the disciplines of prayer and the power that comes through the life of someone who is obedient to calling on Him during all of life's challenges. Gail has firsthand experience in how to develop and build a powerful prayer life; her life is a living testimony of a life transformed by the power of prayer and having a heart of worship.

In *Ready to Pray*, Gail pours her heart into the pages of this book, sharing the intimate and hard lessons that God has taught her — the very circumstances that brought her to her knees before the Lord — the very lessons that taught her about prayer, the power of prayer, the need for prayer, and the joy and freedom that is found in worshipping the Lord Jesus Christ.

In serving in ministry with Gail, I discovered quickly how the power of prayer has transformed her life—both through the prayers that others have prayed for her and through the spiritual disciplines that God has taught her in praying for others. I invite you to journey through the chapters of this book at a pace that will allow you to incorporate these disciplines into your daily life. Seek the Lord on the way that He wants you to apply these lessons. Humble yourself and come before the Lord with your heart wide open, ready to learn and grow in Him.

Thank you, Gail, for your heart for prayer and for your desire to help others grow in their spiritual journey, drawing near to the Lord. Truly you are a living example of how prayer changes lives.

Mary Hamrick
Dragonfly Ministries
www.dragonflyministries.com
Vernon Hills, IL

INTRODUCTION

Why this book? Why another book on prayer? What will this book on prayer say differently than the million and one other books on prayer that line the shelves across the nations?

Honestly, I cannot answer that question for you, but I do know that the Holy Spirit ordained you to grab hold of this book on prayer. I am not an expert. I can only say that prayer has truly sustained me as I go through this life and, through it all, God has continued to teach me how to pray and to intercede on behalf of others. Every time I try and run away from this calling of prayer the Lord has placed on my life, I become thirsty for more of His Word and am drawn to pray and intercede for what He reveals to me day and night. Now is the time that He wants all of His children to pray and to intercede for one another. Therefore, my brother and sister in Christ, it is not by mistake you hold a copy of this book in your hands. The Lord our God is calling us to humble ourselves, seek His face, turn from our wicked ways, and then He will hear from heaven and heal the land! Come! Walk with me.

In my previous book, *Ready to Change My Name: a Spiritual Journey from Fear to Faith*, you may recall the second chapter, "Turning Back." In these pages, I shared the number of times the Lord had called my husband and me to follow His will and His way by stepping out on faith following the path He had set before us. Well, it happened again. The Lord called us to plant a church in the summer of 2005. This meant we would leave our home in Northeast Ohio and move to Columbus, Ohio, to plant a church under His leading. And this is how the story begins....

Ephesians 3:14-19 says, "For this reason I kneel before the Father, from whom his whole family in heaven and on earth derives its name. I pray that out of his glorious riches he may strengthen you with power through his Spirit in your inner being, so that Christ may dwell in your hearts through faith. And I pray that you, being rooted and established in love, may have power, together with all the saints, to grasp how wide and long and high and deep is the love of Christ, and to know this love that surpasses knowledge — that you may be filled to the measure of all the fullness of God."

My reason: To pray that the Lord would see me and Kevin through one of the greatest challenges we had ever faced. Once we completed our move, the hurdles came one after another. First, what would have been steady income for the family to make this transition smooth came to a halt within three months. Immediately, our insurance was cancelled, compensation stopped, and we were left asking God if we misunderstood His vision for our lives. Our standard of living had turned 180 degrees in what seemed like an instant, causing a drastic shift in our finances: our ability to pay our home's mortgage, rent for the church, monthly bills, and the day-to-day cost of living. The bank balance declined quickly and by Christmas, I had no other choice but to pray!

Through prayer, the Lord was already at work, revealing His plan. Fortunately, as a native of Columbus, Ohio, I have the ability to connect with many people, groups, and organizations. However, one day while reading the neighborhood newspaper, I came across an article that read, "Christian Women's Club." That day, I e-mailed the person listed in the article. She immediately responded by inviting me to attend that evening's gathering. As I sat there that evening, I immediately connected with one of the speakers, Erin Campbell, visionary of Water Through The Word Ministries. God positioned me to sit on her right side at the dinner table. I remember this like it was yesterday. As we talked, our spirits immediately connected. During our conversation and sharing, she said, "This outreach group's home office in Kansas City has openings for field directors and I think you would be great." A few days later, I looked them up on the internet and contacted the office. The Human Resources staff person told me where to submit the application and resume, as well as the deadline for all applications for the position. Of course, the deadline was THAT day!

Potential opportunities were coming Kevin's way, but time and time again, the letters would arrive in the mail stating, "Overqualified." By Christmas, we made the decision to share with our children how we would need to make some changes. Our savings disappeared quickly. We were now behind on all sorts of bills trying to make sure that we at least had mortgage payments for a few months. Promises for jobs were coming our way, however, nothing presented itself. People of God, I was scared.

By January 2006, I was in a panic! We had a son in college, a daughter in private school, and a mortgage hanging over our heads. I was led to fast and pray. Allow me to be transparent and say that I was hanging on by a tiny thread which was about to break. I had no idea what would happen to our home, our children's education, our finances, and even our marriage. I gave three days to water and seeking the face of God ONLY. That week, I received a call from Stonecroft Ministries, an international women's ministry where I had applied. They invited me to schedule a telephone interview.

During the telephone interview, I was told that I would hear back either by letter or by phone within a couple of weeks. Within twenty-four hours, I received a call asking if I would be available to come and visit the home office in Kansas City and spend a few days with other applicants. Within two weeks from the visit, I was offered a position as a Field Director. This is power in prayer and it gets better. While interviewing in Kansas City, my husband called me to share a praise report. He said, "While visiting a pastor, he handed me a check." Then he said that our close friends said that they wanted him to focus on building the church and brought a check that would take care of the next month's mortgage. Now, that's God!!! Soon, thereafter, Kevin began working for not just one seminary, but for two. He was also contracted to do ministry development and economic development. God began to move.

I took a step back to ask, "What changed?" The Lord spoke with such powerful words when He replied, "You prayed." In my time of quietness, I realized that I had taken the focus off myself and our situation and instead sought the face of the Lord and His will for our lives. I totally surrendered myself under the leading of the Holy Spirit. If God had decided that the house was not for us, if He had decided that we were to lose everything, I would have been alright. Why? Because I had, for the first time in my life, prayed, "Thy will be done," and actually meant it. So, as Paul says in Ephesians 3:14, "For this reason," my reason was to pray, "Thy will be done, Lord," and mean it. I "kneeled" (the King James Version says *to bow*) to posture myself under the authority of Jesus Christ, who is our Source. Whatever we need, He has the answer.

I positioned myself under His authority and not my agenda. Through my time of fasting and prayer, the Lord strengthened me with power through his Spirit. I can truly say that I gave myself to Christ fully. There was real and authentic dwelling and intimacy with Christ during what I would call my "crisis." When one partakes of His Word and dwells with Him, His love surpasses knowledge. I can pen this book and say that I am filled with a measure of all the fullness of God.

I pray that the information written throughout this book will prompt you to examine your life. I encourage you to utilize the "Steps on the Journey" note section at the end of each chapter to reflect and look within yourself. Pray to God and ask Him to help you examine yourself clearly. Write whatever He instructs you to write. Do not be afraid of the transformation process. I pray this book will lead you to pray with power and authority. I pray that this book will help lead you to recognize when you should fast and pray. I pray that a fresh anointing will fall upon you. I pray that this book will speak life to you. I pray that you will be free to intercede for others. I pray that you will pray for healing and that you will pray with a forgiving heart. I pray that you will have a new prayer walk in the name of Jesus Christ our Lord.

Yes, I have done it again. I have freely shared parts of my life with you in this book. I do it for two reasons. First, with love, knowing ministry is taking place; and secondly, to share how as a pastor, a minister, and as a person who has a passion for prayer, at one point in my life came face-to-face with having to make a decision to pray or not to pray. On one hand, I was ready to give up and had begun to question if my prayers were being heard by God and if He wanted to answer my prayers. I had doubt and many questions. But God! God used me during that time so that I may share with others how to stand on His promises and to never give up praying. God has called me to be transparent. For in my transparency, people will be set free in Jesus' name. We all have a story to tell and it's only by the grace of God that we can tell our story. Satan once again has tried to keep me quiet. He reminded me that my closest friends and family had no idea what I experienced with our financial strain and that we were only holding on by the grace of the Lord. Many times while writing, a negative voice would say, "You don't want anyone to know this about you." However, God would remind me of my freedom in Him. He would remind me as He always does by saying, "*Your testimony is not for you but for you to share with someone else.*" I pray my "freedom" will likewise set you free to pray and to share your story.

As I shared in the introduction of my previous book, "Now that it's out, what can man do to me?" Absolutely nothing! I'm no longer in the dark and I lovingly open the door for you to be liberated to share your story. Now it's your turn to get free and then to set someone else free. I am praying with and for you.

Again, I am not an expert. However, I have lived a life of prayer and the Lord has released me to share my journey with you. Before we jump in and start reading chapter after chapter, I want to share an inside story with you. This isn't a deep book. It's simply a book of my spiritual journey of prayer and worship. A book that I believe will set people free and think about prayer and worship on another level from a real-life perspective. Let's get started!

ARE YOU READY TO PRAY?

Pray with me: Sovereign Lord, we come before You, O God with boldness and under the authority of Jesus Christ! Awesome God, we love You and ask that You would continue to reign upon and within each of our lives, for we are Your beloved children. Heavenly Father, we open wide our mouths so that we may receive all that You have for us. We are ready to feast on Your words. We are ready to walk in Your will and Your way for our lives. Open our ears and our hearts unto You. O God, we pray that You would reveal to us our fleshly desires no matter the pain. God, we also ask that You would forgive us our sins. Lord, today we make the commitment to turn from our wicked ways and walk in the Spirit of God—not the spirit of self. Please deposit a fresh Word unto Your people. Father, we pray You would move suddenly in each of our lives. Let us decrease that You may increase and come forth in our lives with boldness and power. This we pray in the name of Jesus.

I

WHAT IS IT?

What is prayer? Prayer is having a conversation with God. It's talking to Him. It's sharing everything about you with Him. It's crying. It's laughing. It's going to God with your entire heart and talking and talking and talking. It's about coming away with His heart and trusting all He shared with you. It may be a word. It may be peace in your spirit. It may be a still, small voice. It may be a Scripture you have read. It may be silence.

Do you recall your first crush? Remember talking on the telephone for a very long time? Remember forgetting about doing the dishes, cleaning your room, and doing your homework just to talk on the telephone to your newfound love? We would talk so long that a parent or sibling would pick up the telephone to signal to us that our time was up. We would tie up the telephone line for so long that somebody would have to call the operator to interrupt our call. This is when we had only one telephone line and the phone itself was mounted on the wall with a really long cord. Our only option was to stand next to the phone or pull the cord around the corner of the kitchen. This was also back in the day when there was no call waiting or caller ID. If someone was on the phone, you got a busy signal. I remember. I remember my mother putting me on telephone punishment because I stayed on the telephone too long. I remember that I would sneak to call someone after my telephone curfew. I can remember sneaking on the telephone while in my bedroom and talking to my so-called "love" on the telephone under the covers so no one could hear. I even remember falling asleep while on the telephone because I did not want to hang up and stop our conversation. It didn't matter that no words were being spoken! Do you remember? Remember, we would start with "Hello" then move to what happened during the school day. We would talk about what we would wear the next day and share the things we liked. We would even say things like, "I like you. Do you like me?". Prior to having telephone privileges, we would ask that question on a piece of paper with two boxes and ask the "love of our life" to check the box that was true for them, and we would "pray" that they would check the "yes" box. Do you remember? I remember.

That's what it is like talking with God in prayer. Nothing else matters. Not even when it is silent. The silent time we shared on the telephone with our newfound love is the same sort of silence we have at times in prayer, only so much better. So often, we want to talk nonstop when really we should just sit and listen. There are times when we need to allow for the silence. Just like the times when I would fall asleep on the telephone because no one was talking. That's the silence I am referring to when you are spending time with God. Not the falling asleep part, just the silence part. Only sometimes that happens too! I get to the place of such peace and rest in the arms of Jesus that I doze off momentarily only to awake in an awestruck place, a resting place with Christ.

Prayer is going to God with everything about you and coming away with knowing more about Him. A life of prayer is a life that knows there is someone to talk to and that someone is Jesus. He will never judge you. He will never talk badly about you. He will never use what you have shared with Him against you. He will never put you down. He will always listen to you. He will always do what is best for you. He will even caution you and tell you, "No." You can experience the best conversations with Jesus. He is wonderful to talk with. Really, He is.

In my Bible it says, "If my people, who are called by my name, will humble themselves and pray and seek my face and turn from their wicked ways, then will I hear from heaven and will forgive their sin and will heal their land. (2 Chronicles 7:14)

"If my people who are called by my name, will humble themselves…" If we would only first humble ourselves!

Humbling ourselves is a posture; a position of submission. When we do this, God will hear.

When thinking back to our transition to Columbus, I realized that for me, personally, I was not in a posture of submission. I had **my** own plan, **my** own thoughts, and **my** own way of doing things. I was busy trying to hold on to something that God really wanted me to let go of in order to see Him move in our lives. I had to let go of my way in order to make room for His. Yes, the transition was challenging, but I would not trade that experience of seeing the Lord guide our paths for anything. Yes, it was a painful experience, but during that time I was being strengthened in Jesus and building a more authentic relationship with Him.

I had to learn a posture of rest. I had to learn to rest in Christ. To rest, according to Merriam-Webster, is to "have a freedom from activity or labor." Today, I am calling you to rest in Christ. The Word of God says, "He who dwells in the shelter of the Most High will find rest in the shadow of the Almighty." (Psalm 91:1) To rest in the shadow of the Almighty means to let go. Don't worry. Do not wrestle against flesh and blood. It is a place of peace of mind and spirit. Free yourself to think on things that are true, pure, lovely, and of a good report. To worship God is to rest in Him. When we rest in the Lord, there is sweet peace. When we rest in God, we can breathe. When we rest in Christ, we can pray and seek His face.

In 2 Chronicles 7:14, God also tells us to "turn from our wicked ways." This is where God is telling you and me to stop doing things that are not satisfying to Him. In going to God in prayer, I encourage each of us to confess our sins to Him and go to Him with a pure heart and a right spirit. If there is any unrighteousness or unforgiveness, deal with it. Take it to the Lord in prayer. I've been there. I have been in the place of trying to pray with an unforgiving heart. I did not want to let go of how I felt about what others had tried to do to me, my family, and our ministry. I would begin to pray but then slip into the old thought process of my past. Did God hear? Yes, He did. However, I first had to deal with my stuff. God will reveal the areas in your life that need deliverance, healing, and restoration. I had to ask for the Lord's forgiveness. I also had to forgive myself. It's not an easy road, but it is well worth it in the end.

What is it? Prayer is going to God totally open and available to hear, "Thus saith the Lord." More importantly, one must be obedient to all He speaks into your spirit. Prayer is having an open and honest conversation with Jesus. Prayer is a way of life.

STEPS ON THE JOURNEY

Why do you pray?

Because God is my friend. I want to
come to Him. I pray because I need
God's help - God moves thru prayer

Do you believe God will answer your prayers? Why or why not?

Yes, but sometimes he is silent.
For years - on a subject.
Sometimes there's never a move-
ment of God - at least that
I can see

Are you ready to develop a more intimate prayer life with Christ?

How will your prayer life change after reading this chapter?

I need consistency in my prayers.

_____

_____

_____

_____

_____

_____

_____

_____

_____

What will your new prayer life mean to you?

_____

_____

_____

_____

_____

_____

Let's pray.

Father, in the name of Jesus, teach me to pray as You would have to me pray.

"FOR THIS CAUSE, I BOW..."

Ephesians 3:14 (KJV)

Have you ever wanted to talk to someone who can really assist you in your problems? Now, we all have those friends who really are nice and cool and come to us for advice, but how many people do we really know who we can run to them for an ear, a voice, and if I may...love? It comes to a point in life where what we are going through is more than what we went through and, of course, it is more than what we can handle. Tired of being there for everyone else but when it is your time, no one is available?

You may not want to meet with the pastor or a minister for fear of judgment and criticism. You may not want to talk to your parents or family because you know a million and one questions will be asked. Not to mention that you cannot voice your concerns about that person to that person. So, honestly, who can you run to? Allow me to let you in on a secret. Prayer. Oh, the term may have some bad feelings attached to it, but I guarantee you will feel better once you finish. Any time you feel like you want to talk, just begin talking to Him. Catch Him up on your life and how you feel about what is happening. He does care about you and more importantly how you are feeling!

You may wonder: should I pray? Why? And, more importantly, how do I pray? It does not matter your background, it does not matter what you did or how long it has been since you have been to church. You want a change? Are you tired of the HELL breaking loose? Pray. Just talk to God like you want to be able to talk to your friend. Unlike your friend, He will listen, and yes, He will understand. He will not judge you or decide to walk away when you disappoint Him. Don't believe me? Try it. What do you have to lose?

I heard the voice of the Lord, saying: "Whom shall I send, and who will go for Us?"

Then I said, ***"Here am I! Send me."*** (Isaiah 6:8)

—Elder Melvin D. Wilson, Jr.

II

PRAYERLESSNESS

In order to be "Ready to Pray," one must deal with prayerlessness. One day, while speaking with an intercessor in Boston, we shared about the hardened hearts of individuals when it comes to prayer. Oftentimes while facilitating prayer workshops across the country, I am asked the question, "Why are my prayers not being answered?" Although we are taught early in our life never to answer a question with a question, sometimes you have no choice but to ask questions in order to get to the root of the issue. Therefore, my response to the question is to always ask a question, and more often than not, follow-up questions. The first question I ask is: "Is there any unforgiveness in your heart?" and the second question I ask is: "Are you sure God has not answered you and you are avoiding His answer?" It's amazing to me how many people will simply walk away.

Another question that is asked often is, "Why is prayer hard work?" Let me be real. I don't always feel like praying. I'm not sure I consider it hard work or not, but there are times when I simply don't feel like it. I know what I may be doing is totally outside of God's will; therefore, I would rather not pray because, without a doubt, His answer will be different than what I want to hear. Other times my "would be" prayers would not line up with the Word of the Lord. Yes, I, a pastor, a minister, a teacher of the Gospel of Jesus, am not always obedient to the leading of the Holy Spirit to pray. How's that for teaching about prayer and living life based on the importance of prayer? There are times when I am in my self-absorbed mode, having a moment of "all about me," when I do not feel like praying. "Let me be," I've said as I throw myself a pity party with the theme, *"Woe Is Me."* Even if I were to pray in such times, the prayers would only hit the ceiling like an overdone loaf of bread.

As I have responded to others in reference to the reasons their prayers may not be answered, I must ask myself the same questions. Yes, at times there is unforgiveness in my heart. Am I supposed to forgive someone who has hurt me in order to pray for them, myself, and others? Yes, but guess what? I don't feel like it. I want to hold on to my fleshy views and feelings. Selfishly, I want time to be angry and I really don't feel like forgiving someone who has caused distress in my life for no apparent reason. I'll pray as long as I can pray for the Lord to teach them a lesson! Seriously, this is how I feel about prayer at times.

I am just keeping it real with you. Hear me when I say, there are times where we won't feel like praying, but that is just the right time to say, "Jesus, today I don't feel like praying but...." Press through! Want freedom? Release the unforgiveness. It is not worth it and it will cause great pain to you in the long run as well as a broken relationship with Jesus. Jesus came to bring life and an abundant life — live a life free in Jesus. Get over yourself and pray.

The next question that I ask others when they are experiencing what seems to be a "no reply" to their prayers is, "Do you give time in daily reading the Word of the Lord and taking time for quiet meditation?" I'll answer that one as well. Not always. I simply don't make time. I would guess that you didn't expect me to answer that way, did you? I write this book to speak truth. I'm not trying to give you the same old "this is what you are supposed to do" manual. No, I want to speak truth and tell you what I have experienced in my prayer life. Yes, as a pastor who pastors alongside of my husband, I have issues, real issues, too. I'm not walking around with my hands lifted and my voice speaking, "Oh great and mighty God. How excellent is Your name on High," all day, every day. Once again, "Oh, get over yourself!" I'm real and there are times that I put other things before time of prayer, studying the Bible, and sitting somewhere quietly waiting on a divine appointment! Here's the truth — you don't always put time with God first either. Now that we have that out of the way, let me offer an ounce of wisdom. Each of us needs to put forth a real effort to spend daily time studying the Word of the Lord as well as creating time for quiet meditation. How can we pray if we're not in the Word? We can't. All prayers are already written out in the Bible. It's a matter of taking time to study and meditate on His Word both day and night. That's when our prayer life will turn from prayerlessness to prayers with power.

In sharing with other intercessors, we find that some hearts are hardened towards prayer because it is hard work that requires self-sacrifice. As intercessors pray on behalf of another, we are constantly pouring ourselves out and standing in the gap for people. We're always giving of ourselves. One intercessor on our team stated that, "In teaching or having a conversation about prayer to anyone who is not passionate about or interested in prayer, it's important to highlight the sin element of prayerlessness and Jesus' exhortation to pray." In the Bible, the sin element is found in 1 Samuel 12:23, when Samuel said to the children of Israel, "As for me, far be it from me that I should sin against the Lord by failing to pray for you. And I will teach you the way that is good and right." If I fail to pray for you, that's sin. Throughout any given day, the Lord will place names or situations before me. When He does, I am called to pray. There are times when I would rather go about my day without giving thought to lifting up a prayer. However, I would be disobedient to the leading of the Holy Spirit and that positions me as being in prayerlessness. Prayerlessness is a sin and when we are idle or disobedient in praying, we are sinning.

Jesus' exhortation to pray is found in Luke 18:1: "Then Jesus told his disciples a parable to show them that they should always pray and not give up." Jesus did not *suggest* that we pray. He told his disciples and He is telling us that we should *always* pray and not give up. Yes, even when we are tired, weak, and worn, we must pray.

A great starting point is to make the admission that you are not always obedient when the Holy Spirit impresses on your heart to pray. The second step will be to answer, "What shall I do about this?" Go to God and speak honestly about your disobedience. What is prayerlessness? Is it a weakness? Is it a sin? It is important to seek God for His answer to this question. For some, it may be perceived as a weakness, and for others, it may mean that you have little faith and therefore, lack strength and power to rely solely on Christ. It could also mean that you need to spend more time in the Bible and become grounded in the Scriptures. When we look at prayerlessness as a weakness, individuals may take it upon themselves to pray in their own strength and walk in the flesh. The Bible says that we should pray, "Thy will be done." When we pray in our strength, our prayer very seldom changes the situation. This results in sin. This brings about frustration and the desire to stop praying.

Prayerlessness as a sin will call for a different approach. Seeking God's strength is what is needed. Only God can deal with sin. We must confess and surrender our will to His authority. It is as simple as saying, "God, I've sinned and have fallen short." I have found myself naked before

God saying, "Lord, I've messed up. I have not spent time with You and I'm ashamed and ask for Your forgiveness." And He forgives me. One of my ongoing prayers over the years has been this: "God, I desire to be obedient. Help me to be obedient." We deal with our sin in our lives by recognizing the sin, confessing the sin, forgiving the sin, being cleansed of the sin, and finally, repenting of the sin.

The Bible tells us that as Christians we demonstrate our love for our Lord and Savior by our obedience. In the Old Testament, Moses commanded Israel to *"Love the Lord your God with all your heart and with all your soul and with all your strength."* (Deuteronomy 6:5) We read in the New Testament when Jesus speaks the commandment in Matthew 22:37, saying, *"Love the Lord your God with all your heart and with all your soul and with all your mind."* In John 14, Jesus told His disciples in verse 15, *"If you love me, you will obey what I command."* And later in John 14:21, Jesus says, *"Whoever has my commands and obeys them, he is the one who loves me. He who loves me will be loved by my Father, and I too will love him and show myself to him."* God is indeed calling us to love and to obey Him. In loving and obeying God, we freely pray for the individuals and situations that the Lord places before us. Jesus told His disciples in Luke 18:1 that they should always pray and not give up. Paul gives the instruction in 1 Thessalonians 5:17, *"Pray without ceasing."* Prayerlessness is disobedience because as we read the Scriptures, God has commanded us to pray.

"Then Jesus told his disciples a parable to show them that they should always pray and not give up." (*Luke 18:1*)

Oswald Chambers said that "prayer is not preparation for the work; prayer is the work." Prayer is not something that we do when we "feel" like it. Prayer is something that we should always do and never give up. Jesus really does not care that we crowd our calendars with overwhelming workloads and call ourselves "busy." God will work regardless of what is on our plates. Jesus called His temple a house of prayer; we are temples of the Holy Spirit.

Look around and what do you see? I'll tell you what I see through my lenses. I see marriages falling apart. I see children struggling. I see cities going into debt. I see churches preaching a word that only tickles the ear. I see lost people, and the list goes on. Here's a clue: prayerlessness is NOT working. We all know the enemy comes to steal, kill, and destroy, and in looking around, we see that the enemy is busy. It's time to admit that our ways are not working and we need to admit that we've operated in sin and have neglected the call of the Lord. God speaks to us in 2 Chronicles 7:14, "If My people, which are called by My name, shall humble themselves, and pray, and seek My face, and turn from their wicked ways; then will I hear from heaven, and will forgive their sin, and will heal their land."

Please join me in prayer.

Father, in the name of Jesus, please give me Your strength to pray when the Holy Spirit leads me to pray. There are times when I am weak and tired, but I want to be totally obedient to You. Please forgive me for all of my sins. Your Word says to pray without ceasing. There are many who need a prayer covering. I desire to be a vessel that You can use.

"Peace I leave with you; my peace I give you. I do not give to you as the world gives. Do not let your hearts be troubled and do not be afraid." *(John 14:27)*

STEPS ON THE JOURNEY

Have you ever experienced prayerlessness? Explain.

Yes, many times over the years.
Even now.
I get so distracted - find it hard to
concentrate..

Share a time when you asked the question, "Why haven't my prayers been answered?"

When Rob & I have prayed for years
for a business.

How have you handled your prayers not being answered in the past?

I'm sad, can't understand why
Feel God's not caring
Try to stay positive - God's got
his purposes & plans.

Have you ever blamed God for not answering your prayers? Explain.

Yes - sometimes I question His
goodness toward me.

Give details of an account when you began to doubt God due to your prayers not being answered based upon how you wanted your prayer to be answered.

Write out a prayer of forgiveness:

"For This Cause, I Bow..."
Ephesians 3:14 (KJV)

"I was taught to pray."
Alexander M. Roseboro-Dudley

"Pray without ceasing."
I Thessalonians 5:17 (KJV)

I pray because I have been taught to. I pray also because I believe it connects me with God. When I first began to pray, I would pray in the morning when I awoke and at night before I went to bed. As I have matured in my faith, I have begun to understand and embrace Paul's suggestions of praying without ceasing and to pray at all times in the Spirit. Therefore, I have learned through practice how to pray beyond designated times such as when I wake up or go to bed. I have learned to the point where the Holy Spirit leads me to pray while driving, walking, etc. I have also made it a point, as God has led me, to pray when I feel a burden such as a name or person that comes to my thoughts. As I have grown in my relationship with God, I have also found my conversations with God to become more and more complete. I have also discovered that it does not take many words to pray. All it takes is a willingness to talk with God. I am so grateful to God that I do not have to sound a particular way in order to talk with God. It is good to know that when no one else may be listening to what I have to say, God is. And how do I know? By faith, I usually see results. Sometimes the results are not what I had intended, yet God did respond.

— Alexander M. Roseboro-Dudley

III

MORE THAN WORDS!

Prayer is more than words! Prayer is worship. Prayer is a lifestyle. I once heard, "Prayer is when you go to God with your heart and come away with His." As a child I remember reciting these words, "Now I lay me down to sleep...." Later in life, I would find myself praying while washing dishes. I would whisper a prayer before getting out of bed. In the evening I would ask myself, "Did I pray today?" All I knew was that I needed to pray. That was the right thing to do, of course. However, I quickly learned that I was simply saying words. I had formed a habit: a habit of prayer.

I began to seek God for more. I didn't want to form a habit of prayer. I wanted to sincerely seek Christ. I desired an authentic and intimate personal relationship with Jesus. It wasn't immediate, but I began to share my heart, my tears, and my desires. I had graduated from reciting words from a piece of paper to praying Scriptures found in the Holy Bible. I encourage you to never allow your prayers to become a routine which boils down to a day-to-day habitual time of bowing your head, closing your eyes, and uttering a few words without any passion. I remember reading somewhere, "That which is routine without passion will become just another thing you do." Let's not "do" Jesus. However, let us become the hands and feet of Jesus and serve through prayer and worship.

In the book of Mark, we read in chapter 1:35, "Very early in the morning, while it was still dark, Jesus got up, left the house and went off to a solitary place, where he prayed." In the chapter "Prayerlessness," I shared that often times while conducting prayer workshops or having prayer summits, I am asked, "Why is prayer such hard work?" It's hard work because you are wide open for attack when you are covering others in prayer. I would like to suggest that when you are interceding on behalf of another you have someone else covering you in prayer.

Prayer is hard work because we are saying, "God, it's all about You." This means, focus is turned off of ourselves and turned to Christ. Many times I have wanted to pray for myself and a life situation but instead I was led to pray for the nations and for people who were dropped into my spirit. There are times I wanted to pray for a financial breakthrough, but the Holy Spirit led me to pray for the finances of a neighbor or a coworker or someone I passed on the streets. There are times when you will have an experience of having a person's name come to mind or having a dream about someone out of nowhere. I personally believe it is a call from the Holy Spirit to pray for that person or situation. Prayer is hard at times because I struggle to pray my will when I must pray the Lord's will.

Let's spend a little more time dealing with unfor-giveness, as I mentioned in the previous chapter. Prayer becomes hard when you really do not want to let that thing go. We get into the posture of "but God...." We come up with reasons to hold on and hold on tight. We get to a place at times of fleshly processing. We get into a space of unholy living. We get into a place of wanting to simply do our thing. I can recall a time when I sat in church on the front row and hoped for the service to end quickly. I remember being around a person who was praying and as they prayed, I sat there becoming very frustrated because they were taking way too long. I was convicted that day — too long for whom? Jesus takes time with us every second of every minute — He is available all the time. How dare I trip about someone taking their time to pray? How else was I convicted? The person took time out and prayed for me. They prayed the exact prayer I needed. Only the Holy Spirit revealed to them what to pray for me. Prayer is more than words. It's get-ting in a space to receive what the Lord God Almighty has for you. Prayer takes time.

Prayer is a time commitment. Prayer is more than words. Prayer is finding that special place to have com-munion with God. "But when you pray, go into your room, close the door and pray to your Father, who is unseen. Then your Father, who sees what is done is secret, will reward you." (*Matthew 6:6*)

Remember the index cards we used and our so-called "Cliff Notes?" Those short and handy 3x5 note cards that we used as our study guide and to write out our notes to read from? When it comes to prayer, Jesus laid out everything you need to know in Matthew. He gave us step-by-step details on how to pray, how not to pray, and the essentials of forgiveness. Jesus taught His disciples how to pray in Matthew 6:5-13 (KJV):

⁵And when thou prayest, thou shalt not be as the hypocrites are: for they love to pray standing in the synagogues and in the corners of the streets, that they may be seen of men. Verily I say unto you, they have their reward.

⁶But thou, when thou prayest, enter into thy closet, and when thou hast shut thy door, pray to thy Father which is in secret; and thy Father which seeth in secret shall reward thee openly.

⁷But when ye pray, use not vain repetitions, as the heathen do: for they think that they shall be heard for their much speaking.

⁸Be not ye therefore like unto them: for your Father knoweth what things ye have need of, before ye ask him.

⁹After this manner therefore pray ye: Our Father which art in heaven, Hallowed be thy name.

¹⁰Thy kingdom come, Thy will be done in earth, as it is in heaven.

¹¹Give us this day our daily bread.

¹²And forgive us our debts, as we forgive our debtors.

¹³And lead us not into temptation, but deliver us from evil: For thine is the kingdom, and the power, and the glory, for ever. Amen.

May I suggest that we remember two things about prayer? First, God is sovereign and can do as He chooses. Second, Jesus Christ suffered, died, and was raised from the dead and lives today, and for that we have victory for He is victorious. As children of God, we don't have to talk just to be talking. Sometimes, we just need to sit with God and be in His presence. Read Matthew 6:5-15 once more. We read in these few verses the following: praise, participation, petition, penitence, and profession. We read "Hallowed by Your name" and "Yours is the glory." That is praise. We read "Your kingdom come" and "Your will be done on earth." That is participation. We read "Give us today" and "Deliver us from evil." That is petition. We read "Forgive us." That is penitence. And, finally, we read "Thine is the power." That is profession.

Today, take a moment where you sit reading this book. Pick up your sword, the Word of the Lord, and read the beginning of Matthew 6. Read again what Jesus has to say about prayer. In Matthew 6:7, we read, "And when you pray, do not keep on babbling like pagans, for they think they will be heard because of their many words." This may be difficult, but learn to simply sit in His presence. When I was younger, I remember playing a game that involved being quiet. The first person to speak would immediately be counted out of the game. It is amazing how every time someone would either start talking or laughing, soon everyone else would join in the fun. As parents, we try to manipulate our children by saying, "If you sit here for the next thirty minutes without talking, I will buy you ice cream." The things we do to get someone to be quiet! Well, I can only imagine God wanting us to be silent so that He can speak to us during our prayer time with Him. I find myself going on and on and on not saying much of anything at all. I'm sure I don't know what I am saying. If we would be honest, we have all gone to the Lord in prayer just to say, "We've prayed."

Then we have the other extreme. Fear of opening ourselves in prayer. We are so afraid to share our heart that we break into a cold sweat as if we are making a presentation in front of a group of ten thousand. Our heart starts beating fast and hard, we wring our hands, and we may even start shaking, afraid to speak, thinking that we may say the wrong things. We act as though there is some sort of formula. Maybe you are not so eloquent. You get all tongue-tied when you're trying to speak from your heart. I think about the times where I have to have a serious conversation with my family. I know the conversation may cause another pain, but it's a conversation that cannot be avoided. That is a conversation which is difficult to have, but it is required in order to share your heart.

On the other hand, perhaps you are comfortable with words and speak with ease. The words simply roll off your tongue with grace. However, you still are wondering if your prayer will sound like the prayer of another. Come on—let's be honest. We size up the person who goes before us and wonder if we'll get the same "Amen" as the first person who prayed. Stop trying to be so deep. God is not looking for long unpronounceable words or flowery words. The Lord our God wants to have a simple, honest conversation with you. Simply say what's on your heart. Sometimes, it is simply saying "Jesus." Behind the name of Jesus is power, anointing, deliverance, protection, healing, provision, breakthrough, relationship, and the list goes on and on.

Sit down with Him and have a conversation. Imagine sitting across the table from Jesus, sharing your heart. Take a sip of your tea, lean forward, and rest in the shadow of the Almighty God. Speak. Then listen. Be still and know that He is God. Prayer is more than words. It is a real relationship with Christ.

Let's be ready to pray.

Father, in the name of Jesus, I want more with You. I want a relationship where we have more than my words. I want to hear from You, what You desire out of my life. I want to be real and authentic with You even if that means I simply come to You and sit and be silent. Help me to have more than words with You In Jesus' name, I pray.

STEPS ON THE JOURNEY

What are your thoughts about sitting in silence in the presence of the Lord?

_____

_____

_____

_____

_____

_____

What difference does it make (or would it make) in your life if you gave the entire floor to Jesus as you prayed?

_____

_____

_____

_____

_____

_____

_____

What if anything is causing you to shy away from praying in front of others?

_____

_____

_____

_____

_____

_____

Here's a challenge for you. Start today and pray for three minutes and be silent for five for the next week. After one week, write out the difference in your prayer life.

_____

_____

_____

_____

_____

_____

_____

After reading this chapter, what do you believe, if anything, you need to change with your prayer life?

_____

_____

_____

_____

_____

_____

_____

_____

_____

_____

_____

_____

_____

_____

_____

_____

"For This Cause, I Bow..."

Ephesians 3:14 (KJV)

Why Pray?

As long as I can remember, my mother has opened her Bible in the early morning hours, spending what I called her "prayer time" with the Lord. And I used to think to myself, "What could she possibly have to say every day to God? Is God really listening to her? Is He really paying attention to this one woman's small voice while the world's issues are so big?" I used to think that prayer was reserved for "real" suffering, for surviving the unbearable, for someone truly in need...how could I possibly approach Almighty God with my petty problems and my selfish desires?"

Eventually, it dawned on me that those early mornings were just part of my mom's normal prayer "life" and not just time she set aside out of obligation. Fast forward twenty years—I am happy to report that I, too, am living in prayer, because of God's faithfulness. He has continually shown me that my simple words are like no other in His ear, whether I'm just checking in or questioning why or giving thanks or interceding on someone else's behalf. I am eager to seek Him, to recognize the voice of His Spirit, to experience His promises, and to be in His presence. Yep, little old me.

—Becky Jacobson, *Photographer for* Ready to Pray

IV

COME AWAY WITH GOD'S HEART

More often than not, we run to Jesus out of pain and frustration. We think of prayer when we've hit a rough place in life and need God to give us an answer quickly. I tend to be very transparent in my ministry and will use my life as a case study. Allow me to expose myself to share this heart message with you. There have been many times early in my walk with Christ where I would enter into my time of prayer with the Father and wonder why nothing was happening. I couldn't understand the emptiness and the pain I was feeling. I would become frustrated and ready to put Christianity aside, thinking that I must have entered into something that was not real. I became confused and felt alone. I remember having my son, as many would announce, "out of wedlock," and would ask God why Christians placed this label upon me. I remember trying to become a part of activities within the church only to be overlooked by people who were labeled "without sin." My anger grew partly because I knew that although one may not be able to look at the person and see their sin—they had sinned. Everyone has.

Based upon my personal needs, I grabbed my Bible, made myself a prayer closet, and purchased a prayer shawl. I gathered names and requests in a prayer journal only to discover that my fleshly preparation did not make a difference in my prayer life. I was preoccupied with anger and unforgiveness which clouded communication with Christ. I was desperate. In frustration, I said to the pastor's wife, "Okay, during the invitation to give my life to Christ, I was told to receive Jesus in my heart." Been there—done that. So why isn't it working? I will never forget her words: "Search me, O God, and know my heart; try me, and know my thoughts." "WHAT???" I asked. "Search me for what and why try me? I have already been tried!" At that moment, I am not sure if she realized I was about to lose my mind or what, but she took me by my hands and said, "In Psalm 139:23, the Bible tells us to ask God to search us." She continued by saying, "Gail, you have a heart problem. You are going to God in prayer with the wrong attitude, with anger and unforgiveness. Actually that is pretty selfish." Talk about being slapped—even without a hand hitting me across my face!

This is when my life, my prayer, and worship life began to change. You know, every now and then, we need someone bold enough to give it to us straight. Let me stop right here for one moment, take a detour, and say that we can only be bold with individuals that we have a relationship with. This is not to be tried with just anybody you run into. Unless the Lord truly directs you to be bold, simply pray and wait for God to direct you. Now, let me get back to my point. She talked to me as if I were one of her very own children and she was being used by God to answer the very prayer I had been asking of Him. You must exercise wisdom, as this pastor's wife did, when you are being led to speak with boldness into the life of another. Remember, speak life and not death.

What a wake-up call to ask God to search me and to know my heart. He began to show me my heart and it was one ugly sight. I had a real heart problem. As I allowed God to search me, I realized that I needed to release the pride. I had to come clean with many of my secret issues and ask trusted individuals to pray with me. I had this "safe place" in which I was comfortable only sharing the good days and the successes, never revealing the difficult days of raising a son outside of marriage, barely making it on my career path, and still living under my parent's roof, not yet able to show the world that I could "make it." I needed to prove to the world that my son would not be one of the negative statistics of single parenting. I had a chip on my shoulder that someone really needed to knock off. Well, I am here to tell you that between my pastor's wife and Jesus, the chip is nowhere to be found.

So you are probably sitting there thinking, "What does this have to do with prayer and coming away with

God's heart?" I'll tell you. Until you deal with the junk in your heart and release your pride, your prayers will be delayed and your frustration will grow. As I mentioned earlier, I was not comfortable asking people to pray for me because that would mean I would have to give them something to pray about. I was not prepared to reveal my issues. In the introduction of this book, I shared the challenges my husband and I faced during our move to Columbus to plant the church. I remember my father asking me if everything was alright. With my mask on my face and a lie in my voice, I replied, "Sure, everything is fine. Why do you ask?" I put up such a front that he shook his head and said, "I'm sorry, I was under the impression that you all were having some challenges. I must have been mistaken." It wasn't until I returned to my car that I cried like a baby. I knew he could have helped us, but I refused to tell him our issues. It wasn't until I prayed "Thy will be done" and meant it, that I was free from my heart issues. It didn't matter anymore who knew what. God had to break me in order for me to come away with His heart. If you are keeping track I'm sure you are probably asking yourself, "How long has she been a Christian?" Yes, it's a process, my friend. It is a process. The story I shared with you about my pastor's wife was over twenty years ago. When I first prayed, "Thy will be done" and meant every word, it was only four years ago from the publishing of this book. It is indeed a process. There are moments when you think you have conquered something only to find yourself right back where you were before. This heart thing is serious. The heart isn't anything to play with.

In order to be *"Ready to Pray,"* we have to get to a place where we are able to pray and come away with God's heart, not ours. It is not about our individual needs, but about God's heart. What does He want? How can I be obedient to His will for my life? The story of David in the Bible is one of the most powerful stories. We find in the Amplified Bible in 1 Samuel 13:14 these words, "But now your kingdom shall not continue; the Lord has sought out [David] a man after His own heart, and the Lord has commanded him to be prince and ruler over His people, because you have not kept what the Lord commanded you." We read later in Acts 13:22, "After removing Saul, he made David their king. He testified concerning him: I have found David son of Jesse a man after my own heart; he will do everything I want him to do." God calls us to dwell with Him, but how can we dwell with Him when our heart and His heart are not the same heart?

Ephesians 3:16-18:

> *[16]I pray that out of his glorious riches he may strengthen you with power through his Spirit in your inner being, [17]so that Christ may dwell in your hearts through faith. And I pray that you, being rooted and established in love, [18]may have power, together with all the saints, to grasp how wide and long and high and deep is the love of Christ."*

We start out on the right track by receiving Jesus into our hearts the moment we accept Christ. Somewhere during our journey we tend to go solo with our lives instead of living with God's heart. It's amazing how some individuals use God for their momentary fulfillment and only commune with Him when they have encountered a crisis or have an emergency. Jesus desires to dwell completely in our heart and not the piece we decide to hand over to Him. Christ desires to fill us with His glory and He desires to commune continuously with us. Jesus says in John 15:5, "Yes, I am the vine; you are the branches. Those who remain in me, and I in them, will produce much fruit. For apart from me you can do nothing." (*John 15:5, NLT*)

Coming away with the heart of God means you are transformed into a new person. You no longer have your old mucky heart, but you have the heart of Christ. The Bible says in 2 Corinthians 5:17, "Therefore, if anyone is in Christ, he is a new creation; old things have passed away; behold, all things have become new." Living with revelation knowledge in Christ changes our old mindset of who we used to be. It is in Christ where His heart becomes our heart. God is calling us to come away with His heart.

Pray with me.

> *Father, may I dwell with you at all times. Lord, search me, O God, and know my heart. Try me and know my thoughts. And see if there be any wicked way in me and lead me in the way everlasting. Lord, I desire to be so close to You that when I come to You with my heart in prayer, I come away with Your heart.*

STEPS ON THE JOURNEY

Ask God to search your heart. Write out what God speaks to you.

_____

_____

_____

_____

_____

_____

_____

_____

_____

_____

_____

Write out your anxious thoughts.

_____

_____

_____

_____

_____

_____

_____

_____

_____

_____

Commit to having a heart after God. Write in the space below a prayer to God based upon what you've read in this chapter.

_____

_____

_____

_____

_____

_____

_____

_____

_____

_____

_____

_____

_____

_____

_____

_____

_____

_____

_____

_____

_____

_____

_____

_____

_____

_____

_____

"FOR THIS CAUSE, I BOW..."
Ephesians 3:14 (KJV)

"Prayer Is Relationship"
The Prayer That Changed the Life of Lisa Crum

Does God really exist? Why would a loving all-powerful being allow such hurt in the world? What difference does God or no God mean to me?

These questions represented the essence of my search for truth for six years. Oh, I prayed, but I never heard what I wanted or expected to hear. It seemed no one could answer my questions with anything more than "Sunday School answers." You know the kind of answer that people spout off like it is common sense, but when you ask for a deeper explanation they get defensive because they don't know why they believe what they believe? They know about God, but they haven't experienced His presence.

The day came when it was finally time to turn completely away from God or open my mind to the fact that my expectations of Him were wrong.

I met with a couple who would not argue. They simply listened. After a few visits attempting to dispute the authenticity of Scripture with them, they invited me to pray. Feeling defeated in the debate arena, I skeptically agreed to give prayer one more chance.

"God, if You are real, take away my doubts." That was it. Short and simple. No tears. No earthquake of emotion. My doubts were gone.

Since that day in 1989, my life has been an adventure with God. I've had plenty of ups and downs, but I've never again doubted His existence. He is always with me. I never know for sure how He will speak to me, but it usually begins with me taking time to give Him my undivided attention in quiet prayer.

Why Do I Pray?

When I pray, the Creator of everything in heaven and on earth and under the earth speaks directly to me — to me! Who would want to pass on that privilege?

Communicating with the Creator gives meaning and purpose to my existence. I am not a disposable piece of art. I have been given life to interact and participate with the purposes of the One who created me. (*2 Peter 1:3-4*)

My physical birth created the connection for a relationship with a mother and father. Being made in God's image, my existence includes the ability to connect with God in intimate relationship because of His likeness in me.

I have found God is faithful. The choice for relationship is mine. Therefore, I pray.

In that experience of talking with the Creator, the love He placed in me grows and then flows to those around me. The comfort and the adventure for daily life that comes from that love is an experience worth praying for.

— Lisa Biggs Crum
Grow2Sow Consulting, Powell, OH
www.grow2sow.wordpress.com

V

WHEN YOU DON'T KNOW WHAT TO DO

B race yourself! If you are not an early riser, this statement may mess you up! Here it goes. "Rise early!" That's the answer. Hold on and allow me to exegesis a couple of Scriptures. Before you ask, "exegesis" is a critical explanation or analysis, especially of a text. Let's move forward.

In the Bible, we read in the book of Psalms, King James Version, "O God, thou art my God; early will I seek thee: my soul thirsteth for thee, my flesh longeth for thee in a dry and thirsty land, where no water is; To see thy power and thy glory, so as I have seen thee in the sanctuary. Because thy lovingkindness is better than life, my lips shall praise thee." (*Psalm 63:1-3, KJV*) Also, in the book of Proverbs we read, "I love them that love me; and those that seek me early shall find me." (*Proverbs 8:17 KJV*)

Yes, I am suggesting that you rise early and spend time with Christ. I have found my early time with the Lord to be an experience of solitude, thanksgiving, praise, worship, and a time to release all my concerns and worries. Giving praise and thanks to the Lord erases the pain because I find that I turn my focus to the goodness of Jesus. When we turn our thoughts to His thoughts, life situations do not change but our attitude adjusts. In reading the Holy Scriptures we find these words, "It is good to give thanks to the Lord, and to sing praises to Your name, O Most High; To declare Your lovingkindness in the morning, and Your faithfulness every night." (*Psalm 92:1-2, NKJV*)

As we look at the aforementioned three Scriptures, we find these words: lovingkindness, praise, early, and morning. I cannot imagine a more suitable time for praising God than in the morning. We just made it through the night—the darkest hour. Hmmmm, I just said something. Listen; to wake in the morning is truly something to shout about. Go, run tell God how thankful you are and begin to sing praises unto His name! It's that simple. Once you begin to sing praises and tell Him "Thank You," you find that the situation becomes small in comparison. Yes, at five o'clock in the morning time, it's still somewhat dark on the outside, but I go to my quiet place in the living room and open the blinds to get a glimpse of the morning light. As I begin to pray and seek His face, the room begins to brighten with the morning sun. What a mighty God we serve! I continue to praise and offer thanksgiving and find that I no longer have a need to request anything because the sun is shining brightly, meaning the Son is standing in intercession with the Father on my behalf. What a glorious day! Before you ask, no, the situation has not changed, but my mindset has. I no longer look defeated but I walk in victory of Christ. He already has this situation taken care of.

When you don't know what to do, may I suggest that you rise early in the morning with thanksgiving and praise? Could it be that rising early helps us with our life situations throughout the day? That's why we hear the phrase, "Prayer changes things." In the chapter, "Come Away with God's Heart," I speak about going to God with your heart and coming away with His. There's something to this morning thing. As I mentioned before, even when our heart is heavy, releasing our heart to Him frees us of the anxiety within us, the uncertainties, the insecurities, the hopelessness, the oppression and depression, and the concerns of everyday life circumstances. Imagine releasing those things early in your day through praise and thanksgiving and by night declaring your faithfulness. Wow! My Bible says in Acts 13, "By God's grace, remain faithful." (*Acts 13:43b, NLT*) If we are faithful, how would our lives be different?

Recall the lyrics of a song: "Like the dew in the morning, gently rest upon my heart." (*Judith Christie McAllister, "Like the Dew," Send Judah First, Judah Music, January 30, 2001*) Early in the morning, the dew falls as we sing praises and thanksgiving unto our Lord until it saturates our entire being. It's like an offering before the Lord, giving Him our morning's energy, our morning's freshness and passion. Then I hear the words, "All to Jesus I surrender, all to Him I freely give. All to Jesus I surrender, All to Him I freely give. I will ever love and trust Him. In His presence daily live. I surrender all, I surrender all. All to Thee, my blessed Savior, I surrender all." *(Judson W. Van DeVenter)*

Judson W. Van DeVenter the author of "I Surrender All," explains how his own indecision would result in the writing of this hymn. He says,

"For many years I had been studying art. My whole life was wrapped up in its pursuit and the thing farthest from my mind was active Christian service. My dream was to become an outstanding and famous artist. After graduating from college, I studied drawing and painting under a well-known German teacher. To help me financially, I taught school and eventually, I became supervisor of art in the public schools of Sharon, Pennsylvania. It was during this period in my life that a revival was held in the First Methodist Church of which I was a member. I became very interested in these meetings as a personal worker. The Spirit of God was urging me to give up teaching and to enter the evangelistic field, but I would not yield. I still had a burning desire to be an artist. This battle raged for five years. At last the time came when I could hold out no longer and I surrendered all my time and my talents. It was

then that a new day was ushered into my life. I wrote I Surrender All in memory of the time when, after the long struggle, I had surrendered and dedicated my life to active Christian service for the Lord."

Rising early may mean you have to surrender an extra hour of sleep. Rising early may mean pushing yourself to "get over it" and praise your way through a rough season. Rising early may mean surrendering your all to Jesus. Whatever the case, you decide if you want to remain in what may be your darkest hour, remain in a long struggle, remain in a state of defeat, or choose to enter into a daily time of intimacy with Jesus by believing the words of the Lord, "I love them that love me; and those that seek me early shall find me." *(Proverbs 8:17, KJV)* Don't you want to find Christ? It requires you to seek Him early and by seeking Him early, you are telling Him that you love Him. You are expressing to Him, "I don't know what to do except to sing praises and to offer thanksgiving to Your name, O Most High God."

Pray with me…

How excellent! How excellent is Your name on high! I love You, Jesus. You are amazing. You are wonderful. You are powerful. You are all knowing. You are God. I lift Your name this day realizing that at Your name, every knee shall bow and tongue shall confess that You are God. I thank You for being God all by Yourself.

I thank You, Father, for standing in the gap on my behalf. I thank You for protecting me and my family. I thank You for allowing me room to mess up at times. I thank You for forgiving me of my sins. I thank You for this time we shared in communion. Thank You, Lord. Thank You!

STEPS ON THE JOURNEY

Do you find it difficult to rise early? Why or why not? Please explain.

_____

_____

_____

_____

_____

_____

_____

_____

_____

Do you find that you are embarrassed to praise God when you know others are near? For example, if you don't live alone, would you be uncomfortable if others woke up and found you praising God? Please explain your answer.

_____

_____

_____

_____

_____

_____

_____

_____

Do you find you are unable to praise God because of a particular situation you are going through? Explain.

_____

_____

_____

_____

What is holding you back?

_____

_____

_____

_____

List at least seven Scriptures of praise and thanksgiving that you can use over the next seven weeks that will move you to an ongoing place of praise and thanksgiving when you don't know what to do.

_____

_____

_____

_____

_____

_____

_____

_____

_____

_____

"FOR THIS CAUSE, I BOW..."
Ephesians 3:14 (KJV)

This is my journey of prayer: My first inkling that I needed to pray came as I realized the Lord's Prayer was JESUS praying. I looked further at the Gospels and saw how Jesus sought God out in prayer and came to the conclusion that if Jesus, God's own Son, needed to pray, I surely did, too!

I guess communication with God came as I read the Bible, particularly the New Testament, and began to really understand God's love for me and how very much I owe Him. That led to my calling on Him for my salvation as He Himself says He is the Only Way to the Father. Praying was a way of thanking Him for leading my life even when I did not seek Him or know Him. As I read the Old Testament and realized this God of Miracles was the same God as Jesus called upon, I came to trust Him as the only One who is capable of keeping every single one of His promises.

As a young believer, I asked God to give me a hunger and thirst for righteousness and He answered my prayer by having a friend invite me to a Bible study in our neighborhood. Through reading the entire Bible for myself, I concluded that there is no one like God, just as He says. There is none who is capable of answering prayer, and even beyond that, of knowing the future, and therefore, discerning what is <u>best</u> for <u>me</u>! Why...I don't even know that! I have come to trust His love and mercy, His wisdom, and grace. I desire to be with Him daily for cleansing, fellowship, direction, and for the reassurance that He hears my cry and records my tears in His record and that He will make all things right some day. I see He also desires to be with me as my call to prayer is FROM HIM in the first place. He draws me to Himself and soothes my turmoil as I listen to Him. He has given me the privilege of lifting others to Him for their salvation, direction, healing, and much more. I am learning that praying His promises acknowledges His worth and agrees with His heart. I see my prayers (like Esther's) can make a difference in my time and my world. I find comfort and encouragement to press on because He <u>values</u> my prayers; they please Him and move Him and focus His mighty power. I envision myself as a bow treader...bending and stringing the powerful bow which will propel my requests upward toward the Throne of His Majesty — a pointer of glory to the One who deserves it.

— Beth Renken, OH

VI

INTERCEDING ON BEHALF OF ANOTHER

There is truly an urgency to pray for individuals, marriages, families, churches, pastors, government, communities, the lost, and our cities. We find in the Bible this passage of Scripture, "One night the Lord spoke to Paul in a vision: "Do not be afraid; keep on speaking, do not be silent. For I am with you, and no one is going to attack and harm you, because I have many people in this city." (*Acts 19:9-19*)

We are called by God to intercede. Intercession is praying and standing in the gap on behalf of another. Believe it or not, everyone has been called to pray on behalf of another. However, God has called others specifically to the ministry of intercession. Intercession is not about your personal conversation with God about yourself, your needs, and your desires. Intercession means standing in the gap, covering, warring, and sometimes weeping on behalf of someone else in prayer. Sometimes it is when the Lord puts the face of a person in front of you or maybe the Lord drops someone's name in your spirit or it could be a vision of a person or a situation that the Lord has given you. There's nothing you can do but pray. Intercession is having a connection with God, talking with Him, petitioning Him, crying out to Him, through prayer on behalf of a need of another.

All across the world there are individuals whom God has chosen to stand in the gap for someone else or for a particular situation. We may not know the person, the ministry, the church, or the organization by name, but He will quicken our spirit to begin to pray in a prayer language to intercede. For example, in October of 2009, the Lord called me to bring together prayer intercessors from across the nations to pray for all children, teens, and young adults. I discerned young people were in trouble and there was an urgent need for prayer. Once we announced the date and the hours of prayer, prayer requests poured in at the level that seriously made many of our hearts weep. There were so many requests that my computer crashed. My e-mail inbox reached an average of three thousand e-mails per day. We solicited intercessory leaders in each city, state, and country. Individual prayers turned into neighborhood prayers and the neighborhood prayers turned into community prayers and the community prayers turned into city prayers. On December 12, 2009, the "Urgent Plea for Prayer" took place with many intercessors coming together for twelve hours to pray and intercede on behalf of young people. In the end, we realized praying for the young people opened the door to transform entire communities, cities, neighborhoods, schools, and even households. Individual people were transformed.

I caution you that when you say you will pray for someone, do so. Intercession should not be taken lightly. Someone's life is may be hanging in the balance and they are relying on God's intercessors to fast and to pray and to intercede on their behalf. Imagine if we start praying for a person as soon as they are born and continue to pray for them until they are graduating from high school. Praying for newborn babies and continuing to pray as these babies grow into preschoolers, school-age students, teenagers, young adults and, eventually, adults. The Lord spoke to Paul in a vision. He told him to keep on speaking and to never be silent. I can only imagine Paul as he operated in the truth, exposing things that were not of God. We have to get to the place to speak the truth and to speak the truth in love and to never be silent. What would happen if you saw or heard something taking place in your immediate community, city, school system, or government, and you began to pray and fast and stand in intercession? How would things and people look different? We need a strategy to stand in one accord and pray without ceasing. Paul, I believe, had a strategy in praying for his city. I believe he prayed continuously. Look at Ephesians 3:14.

Study the prayer for the Ephesians: "For this reason I kneel before the Father, from whom his whole family...." People of God—kneel before the Father. That's kneeling for whatever reason you need to pray. Say it's for your city. Kneel before the Father on behalf of Columbus, Ohio, for example. Be more specific. Kneel before the Father on behalf of the near eastside of Columbus in the lower income area. You can be even more specific. Kneel before the Father on behalf of the elementary school in the near eastside lower income area of Columbus. Get the picture? Then, the Scripture in Ephesians goes on to say, "I pray that out of his glorious riches he may strengthen you with power...." Yes, pray for strength for one another to withstand the attacks and the plots of the enemy. Yes, pray for power—Holy Ghost power. As you continue to read, it says, "...so that Christ may dwell in your hearts through faith." This tells me we have to have faith in our prayers and believe in the truth of the Lord God Almighty. No sense of praying without faith. We have to have faith. Why pray if you do not believe? I'll let you marinate on that for a moment.

This book was birthed to take you on a spiritual journey of prayer and praise. Therefore, I need to be transparent as God has called me to be before we can move forward. While following the plan of the Lord for the need to pray and intercede for young people as I mentioned earlier, I ran into some territorial issues of others. I was amazed at how many ministries and individuals I called who questioned why I was calling for this "twelve hours of prayer," even after sharing my heart and the vision of the Lord to pray on behalf of young people. Some individuals in leadership roles stated, "We pray already — there's really not a need, so why are you calling this gathering?" It was as though there was a locked door on prayer. I began to seek God and asked, "How do I respond to these individuals who are telling me there's not a need for this plea for prayer?" Without a doubt I was quickened in my spirit with these words, "You are building the Kingdom of God. They are building their own individual kingdom. Go forth with what I have called you to do." Enough said — so I moved forward in Jesus' name, for this too becomes a part of interceding on behalf of others. There may be roadblocks ahead of you. Therefore, pray for personal agendas and territorial issues to be broken in, Jesus' name. A part of praying is to tear down strongholds, rid your household, cities, communities, government, schools, and even churches, of idols and to pray for restoration and the presence of the Lord God Almighty.

As individuals are equipped and released to walk in the authority of Jesus Christ, they begin to fulfill the Words of the Lord. We find in Jeremiah where God says, "I am watching to see that My word is fulfilled." (*Jeremiah 1:12*) Like, Jeremiah, God has called us and although we say, "Lord, I do not know how to speak," He responds back to us as He did with Jeremiah by saying, "You must go to everyone I send you to and say whatever I command you." Fear hits us when it is time to intercede on behalf of others. When we pray, we kneel before the Father on behalf of cities, governments, nations, young people, marriages, and we pray for individuals and organizations, we pray for people who have been hurt, who may have caused another pain, we pray for healing, deliverance, forgiveness, and so forth. At times that may bring about fear because we don't want to pray the wrong prayer; or when God speaks to our spirit as He did verbally to Jeremiah, "Do not be afraid for them, for I am with you and will rescue you," we may not want to deliver the message. The Lord is saying to each of us as He appoints us to intercession to cover others in prayer: "Today I appoint you over nations and kingdoms to uproot and tear down, to destroy and overthrow, to build and to plant." Will you be obedient to His call?

We have been ordained for such a time as this to fulfill our intercessory roles in praying and interceding on behalf of another. Pray for the sick, people needing deliverance, the president, his or her cabinet, teachers, parents, counselors, businesses, government, media, arts, education, hospitals, colleges, schools, neighborhood associations, pastors, and churches, and when we do we will begin to see those things that are not of God removed. Stop fretting and start praying. Stop complaining and start praying. I've seen things change after a team and I have interceded on behalf of another and in situations that seem totally impossible. Prayer truly changes things. It may not turn out exactly like you have prayed — that is why it is really important to pray in line with the Word of the Lord and to pray His heart, as I mentioned in previous chapters of this book. We should pray and we should walk in the anointing and in obedience of Jesus, that He will raise up Spirit-filled individuals who will keep watch and pray.

You may be asking, "Can individuals be transformed for Jesus Christ simply by interceding on behalf of another?" I would have to answer, yes. I say that after listening to some of the intercessors during the "Urgent Plea for Prayer" that was held on December 12, 2009. I recall these words by one of the women who prayed, "Reading these requests are the same situations adults face. If we had someone praying for us when we were children we would not be in the state that we are in today." If you look at the book of Acts, we see that one city was transformed. I cannot say if it was due to praying for the young people, but still the city was transformed while people were praying. Over and over again, I see two key ingredients while interceding on behalf of others. Of course, prayer is the number one focus. Through collective prayer we can break strongholds of young people. We can pray for their deliverance, healing, restoration, and God's perfect will. Unity in prayer will shift the spiritual atmosphere. We should pray for young people who are connected to churches, businesses, the education system, within the hospitals, and a part of the arts and entertainment industry. Find the places they attend and begin to walk and pray. Lay hands, speak life, and believe in the power of prayer. One must strategically align themselves with intercessors throughout a city and across the nations for the greatest impact.

Secondly, we must be humbled. The Bible says, "If my people, who are called by my name, will humble themselves and pray and seek my face and turn from their wicked ways, then will I hear from heaven and will forgive their sin and will heal their land." 2 *Chronicles 7:14 (NIV)* God calls individuals who realize they need each other who can set aside their own agendas and do the work of the Lord for His glory. In Psalm 25:9 we read, "He guides the humble in what is right and teaches them his way." We should forgo the egos and pride which often prevent us from coming together in prayer on behalf of another for the purposes of Christ.

Ephesians 6:18 says, "And pray in the Spirit on all occasions with all kinds of prayers and requests. With this in mind, be alert and always keep on praying for all the saints." Through intercession, we stand in the gap in prayer on behalf of another.

I Desire to Pray For You...

Most Holy and Awesome God, how excellent is Your Name in all the earth. The God of love who sits high and looks down below sending blessings and promises to Your people. I pray in the name of Jesus for the person who is holding this book right now. God, only You know exactly what they stand in need of. I lift up to You their very concern, their dreams, and desires. In the name of

Jesus I pray, "No weapons formed against them shall prosper." God, breathe into Your child new life. Open up the windows of heaven and pour them out a blessing that they will not have room enough to receive.

Ephesians 3: 14-19 reads, "For this reason I kneel before the Father, from whom his whole family in heaven and on earth derives its name. I pray that out of his glorious riches he may strengthen you with power through his Spirit in your inner being, so that Christ may dwell in your hearts through faith. And I pray that you, being rooted and established in love, may have power, together with all the saints, to grasp how wide and long and high and deep is the love of Christ, and to know this love that surpasses knowledge that you may be filled to the measure of all the fullness of God."

I speak blessings, love, the power of God, life, anointing, encouragement, and opportunities into your life. I pray the blood of Jesus upon your life. I pray that you are blessed in an unusual way. I pray that your life will never be the same. I pray that one day soon I will hold in my hands a book that your will write and publish. I pray that the many gifts that God has placed on the inside of you will take you to the next level of Kingdom ministry. In the name of Jesus. AMEN!

STEPS ON THE JOURNEY

List names of individuals you believe God has called you to intercede for.

_____

_____

_____

_____

_____

_____

_____

_____

Like Jeremiah, God has called you. He is watching for His Word to be fulfilled. What Word has He spoken to you that you have yet fulfilled?

_____

_____

_____

_____

_____

_____

_____

_____

_____

_____

_____

Write down the names of young people you will commit to pray for the next twenty-one days. List the praise reports after the twenty-one-day prayer period.

_____

_____

_____

_____

_____

_____

_____

_____

_____

If you are interested in learning more about "Urgent Plea for Prayer" prayer gatherings for all children, teens, and young adults across the nations, contact, Ready to Pray at GED@ReadytoPray.info.

"For This Cause, I Bow..."

Ephesians 3:14 (KJV)

Why Do I Pray?

I pray because I'm a Christian.

I pray so I can learn to have a better understanding of who I am in my Christian experience.

I pray to strengthen my relationship with God.

I pray because it makes me feel better.

I pray because I know God will listen to my prayers, and then guide me in the right direction. My faith will also be strengthened knowing He's listening.

I pray because I know God will always be in my life as long as I stay faithful. I will always give him thanks.

— Deacon Richard Williams
Gail Dudley's brother-in-law

VII

IT'S DIFFERENT

The Holy Scriptures say in 1 Samuel 10:6-7, "The Spirit of the Lord will come upon you in power, and you will prophesy with them; and you will be changed into a different person. Once these signs are fulfilled, do whatever your hand finds to do, for God is with you."

Here are words from a minister friend of mine when we were having a discussion about the calling the Lord has placed upon my life in reference to prayer, a ministry of prayer, and how the Lord is positioning me in this season. She said, *"A different spirit, Bishop. You have a different spirit than the rest. You have a different type of ministry, my dear. You are in the international arena, getting prayers answered and getting work done. All I keep hearing is 'different.' Not a bad thing at all. Just know your assignment."* She continued by saying, "Remember, every GOOD work is not a GOD work for YOU. If He doesn't put you in it, you don't belong there. You have to be where you belong in order to be effective for Him." Then she ended by saying, "Nuf said."

Yes, it is different! Many times I wanted to hand this calling of prayer over to someone else. However, God called me to it, so I need to be obedient to His call. I struggled and, at times, still struggle with this call because it is like having people's lives in my hands. But, without a doubt, I know the calling the Lord has placed on my life and a part of this call is intercessory prayer— praying with a team of intercessors. I struggled because I did not want to be responsible for the lives of others. As an intercessor, that is a big responsibility and weight. Haven't you ever encountered someone who asked you to pray and you said, "Sure, I will," only to walk away and within a few seconds totally forget about doing it? It is not that you don't want to pray—you have every intention of praying. It's that you become distracted by the day-to-day agenda items and you simply forget to pray. I never wanted to tell someone I would pray for them only to end up not praying at all. That's why I say at that moment of being asked to pray, "Let's pray now." I grab their hands or touch them on the shoulder and begin to pray, "Our Father...."

The moment I finally understood that God was calling me into the ministry of prayer and in the area of intercession, I said, "Hold up; wait a minute. God, that's a lot of responsibility." I know I am not alone in responding to God in this way. I know you've been there. Have you ever wanted to give up, yelling, "I quit!"? Get to a place where you are ready to throw in the towel? Are you or have you ever questioned your life purpose and your ministry calling? Have you ever doubted God and the calling He has placed upon your life? Ever questioned God by saying, "Hey, do You know who You called? Remember me? I'm the one that cussed. I am the one that had sex prior to marriage. I am the one that lied the other day. I am the one who shared in some gossip. I am the one who turned my back on You when things were not going right. I'm the one who…" (you fill in the blank). At this point, you question if you are doing what you are supposed to be doing. Do you begin something and later question if you are supposed to be doing it? Do you ever find yourself asking God, "Are you calling me?" and He responds, "Yes, I am calling you because you are different—you're exactly who I need for this particular purpose." God is saying, "The ministry I have called you into…. Well, it's different. It's not going to mirror anyone else or anyone else's ministry."

I've stopped many times on this journey of prayer and worship and asked, "God, are You sure?" Many times, I worry that I will fail Him. Talking about living in fear! Fear of messing up what God has called me into. Scary, wouldn't you say? Different! Many of us are facing the world of "different" right now. For whatever reason, different brings about a feeling of incompetent, ill-equipped, unappreciated, undeserving, not good enough, unworthy, and overlooked to serve in your community, ministry, your local church, or any other organization that you may be involved with all because what God has called you into is "different." Can we handle the pressure of being different? Speaking in tongues? Different. Laying hands, especially in a traditional church? Different. Speaking life to someone who is used to hearing death? Different. Sharing a prophetic word? Different. Seeing what God has shown you to come to pass? Different. Being used by God when you are not worthy? Different. It's just different.

Talking about different—I pray differently. People are not used to hearing, "I declare and I degree!" People think I have lost my mind. I have heard people say, "Gail, you are weird." I have become used to being called weird, crazy, whatever. After hearing one of my husband's sermons, I now walk in the authority of crazy. Crazy for God! Meaning, I'm crazy enough to believe God and all that He has called me to. If He said it, then it is so! In the name of Jesus! Now that's boldness! That will take back territory the enemy has stolen. Being that "crazy" to pray and believe God!

There are times when a person will talk at me and try to tear me down and I just look at them and pray for their healing and deliverance. Why healing and deliverance? Because if they are talking to me to rip me up one side and down another without any real reason, they need some deliverance and healing from whatever emotional issue they may be experiencing. See what I mean? I'm different. It's time for you to become different. When you're different and you know it—nothing and no one can touch you. That is walking in God's authority. When He tells you to speak something – speak it. When He tells you to touch – touch. Do everything He tells you to do in Jesus' name.

No, it's not easy. Let me be totally honest with you. I wonder sometimes if I am capable and equipped to do the work that has been given to me. As another may question my ability, I begin to question myself. As we look back over our life, we realize the potential we have to ruin the assignment God has given to you and me. Fear and worry have begun to consume our mind and control our behavior. I have come to the conclusion that many are insecure, full of fear, scared of the unknown, double-minded, self-centered, and perhaps a bit of a "people pleaser," and this is why we fall short in fulfilling our call. We are unsure of the calling that has been placed upon us. When we get to this point, it's only by the grace of God that we don't lose our mind. Have you ever had people question your calling? Have you ever had anyone ask you why you do the things you do? They were not convinced that God really called you. They tried everything possible to turn you away. They interrogated you. They recalled your past to discourage you from continuing. They zoned in on all the reasons why you cannot and should not answer "The Call."

Then it happens. God positions you to speak a prophetic word to someone or to lay hands upon someone as you pass by them in silent prayer. All you remember is what your friends and families have reminded you of—your mistakes and shortcomings. You are now in a posture of fear. I am reminded of this saying by Joyce Meyer, " 'FEAR' is only false evidence appearing real!" Are we operating in a spirit of fear and therefore struggling with our call? Have you ever mouthed the question, "Why me?" Have you ever wondered why God chose you? No one seems to want you around but you know God has specifically called you for such a time as this. You have been prepared. You have all the skills, talents, and spiritual gifts for the ministry opportunity that God is calling you to. However, someone else is always criticizing you and trying to do your job for you. Don't miss this. They are really trying to get you to step aside so that they can step in. Haven't you heard, "What God has for you is for you"? Quitting appears easy, but you know God has charged you with an assignment that cannot be avoided.

You are not alone. We all struggle with our calling. Os Hillman wrote in one of his devotionals, *"In my own life, I knew God called me to certain endeavors. Yet every time I turned around, a roadblock stood in my way. It took years of plodding along before the light came on as to why there was such a distance between what God called me to do and the manifestation of that calling. When David was anointed king of Israel, it was years before he realized the manifestation of that calling. There were a number of reasons for these delays."* (Os Hillman, "God's Double-Talk" Devotional) I say, you may be delayed, but you are never denied!

In the ministry of prayer and intercession, one must exercise wisdom. It is truly easy to bear the burdens of other people's challenges. I can remember after receiving tons of prayer requests, I shared with my cousin, Theresa, "My heart is so heavy. I have been feeling what people have been requesting in their prayers. It is as if I am taking on these people's burdens, illnesses, prayer requests, etc." She responded, "Remember that Jesus is the burden bearer, not you. You are to CARRY the burdens to Him and let Him take care of them. DO NOT TAKE THEM UPON YOUR SHOULDERS." She couldn't leave her comments with those words. The Lord had given her a discernment to also share with me: "With the type of prayer ministry you have, you have to be careful not to let it burden you down. Think of yourself as a courier. You're just carrying it to God. He bears the load and already has answers for everyone." Then she ended her message with such power: "You are not Jesus!" As I mentioned in another chapter, I felt like I was hit without anyone using their hand. But that's not the end of the story. Theresa followed up her message by saying, and it was meant in a stern, but caring way, "We are not supposed to take the place of Christ. We have to know how to care for others without actually taking their <u>stuff</u> upon ourselves." It's different.

I want to share something important with you: *Man did not choose you—God did!* The Bible declares in John 15:16, "You did not choose Me, but I chose you and appointed you that you should go and bear fruit, and that your fruit should remain, that whatever you ask the Father in My name He may give you."

Allow me to pray with you…

Jesus, I realize the ministry You are calling me to is different. Please, Lord, give me the confidence and strength to stand even when others are not in agreement with the path You have placed before me. Lord, help me to surrender my fears. Father, help me to walk in the authority of Jesus Christ, Your Son.

STEPS ON THE JOURNEY

God is pleased with you. He is excited that you are serving the Kingdom of God. Never allow another person to tell you what you can and cannot do. Do you believe that Jesus has already called you to a ministry of prayer? Please explain.

_____

_____

_____

_____

_____

_____

_____

_____

_____

_____

Look closer to your commitment to pray on behalf of others. What is different about you and your ministry of prayer?

_____

_____

_____

_____

_____

_____

_____

How can your being "different" impact the community of Jesus?

_____

_____

_____

_____

_____

_____

_____

_____

_____

_____

_____

Take a moment to reflect. Be honest with yourself and write down the challenges that may be interfering with your ministry of prayer.

_____

_____

_____

_____

_____

_____

_____

_____

_____

Write in this area those things you have been afraid to do as it pertains to ministry. Make a commitment to begin to implement at least one item over the next twenty-one days.

_____

_____

_____

_____

_____

_____

_____

_____

_____

_____

_____

_____

_____

_____

_____

_____

_____

_____

_____

_____

_____

_____

_____

_____

_____

"For This Cause, I Bow..."

Ephesians 3:14 (KJV)

When I first started to pray, I wondered if God could really hear me, as the Bible promises. So I asked God, "If You can hear me, would You send me a sign? Please send a dragonfly as a symbol that You hear me and that you love me." God placed a dragonfly in my path the very next day. When I saw it, I was reminded of the request I had made to God and I immediately knew that it was His way of pouring His love over me. That happened ten years ago, and I no longer ask for signs of His presence because I have grown to know and understand that God indeed hears and answers my prayers.

God promises in the Bible that "if you seek me you will find me, when you seek me with all your heart." I hang onto that promise daily, as I pour out my heart to God in times of trouble and joy, in times of hardship and abundance. Through the power of prayer, I have learned that God is my best friend, my provider, my shepherd, my guide. No matter what I say to Him or ask of Him, He is faithful to hear and answer my prayers. I encourage you to continue to seek God and hold onto His promise that "when you seek Him, you will find Him, when you seek Him with all your heart."

— Mary Hamrick
Dragonfly Ministries
www.dragonflyministries.com
www.awalkwithpapa.com
295 Noble Circle
Vernon Hills, IL 60061

VIII

WHAT IS GOD SPEAKING?

B efore we begin this chapter, allow me to share my heart even more. I hesitate to write this chapter. Why? I do not want anyone taking this chapter as a formula to hearing God. Remember, I am sharing my journey of prayer and worship with you. In a few moments you will have the opportunity to share your spiritual journey of prayer and worship. But for now, I'm sharing, and there may be things that touch you in a special way. You may receive a confirming word or Jesus may speak to you by reminding you of something that will strike a heart cord on the inside of you. You may realize that He speaks to you through silence or in dreams and visions. I only want to make sure that you do not use this chapter as a formula. There is nothing magical about listening. It all has to do with your personal relationship with Christ.

I hear you. You're frustrated because you fear God does not and will not speak to you. That's a lie from the enemy and in the name of Jesus, I send that lie back to the pit of hell!

I'm still one step ahead of you. You're looking to hear God as your best friend describes how He speaks to them. Get over it. That's a totally different relationship. He may <u>not</u> speak to you as He speaks to your friend.

Still ahead of you. You're looking to "dream" the answer. Maybe that's not the gift He has given unto you.

You're looking to have warmth that flows throughout your body. Sorry, that's not for you either.

I must start with the Word! "In the beginning was the Word, and the Word was with God, and the Word was God." *(John 1:1)* Honestly, I can end this chapter right here with the Word!

If that Scripture doesn't grab you, what about, "Be still and know." *(Psalm 46:10)* Anxious? My Bible also says, "Do not be anxious about anything, but in everything, by prayer and petition, with thanksgiving, present your requests to God." *(Philippians 4:6)* God speaks through His Word! Let's break this down. We are often so busy that we miss God speaking. Think about it. You have found a space to call your place of prayer and as soon as you get settled, your mind begins to roam. Before that time of prayer, your mind was not distracting you. Let's go there. We are often distracted and therefore, may not hear God speaking. We have to learn stillness. We have to be confident and "know" He is God. That's what the Scriptures say; "Be still and know."

It never fails. I get into my space of prayer and the telephone rings. Then from there I'm distracted and from there, the day is over. What happened to my time of prayer? I wasn't still. I wasn't confident in knowing that He is God. I had other things on my agenda that I allowed to consume me. Let's keep it real.

Anxious, according to the "Free Online Dictionary," is defined as "uneasy and apprehensive about an uncertain event or matter; worried. Attended with, showing, or causing anxiety." Being anxious becomes a distraction within itself. Look at, Philippians 4:6 once more: "Do not be anxious about anything, but in everything, by prayer and petition, with thanksgiving, present your requests to God." I want to pull out these words; "but in EVERYTHING, by PRAYER and PETITION, with THANKSGIVING, PRESENT your requests to GOD." We are called to present our requests to God. If we are called to present, wouldn't you think He would answer?Come on! God is speaking, but the question is, are you listening?

Oftentimes, I am asked, "Do you hear from God? And if so, what does He say?" What a loaded question! Yes, I hear from God, but it's not always audible. Matter of fact, He usually speaks to me through reading of Scriptures, answering many of my prayers. The Bible says in Jeremiah 1:4 the following, "The Word of the Lord came to me saying...." Notice it says, "The Word of the Lord." God will speak to us at times through His Word. If He at times speaks to us through His Word, we must read His Word. Other times He speaks to me through others with a confirming word. Yes, there are times He speaks audibly, but it is not every day. Stop. Please do not read this chapter looking for a formula for you to hear God. God speaks to each one of His children differently. Here's a real-life example: I speak to my son differently than I speak to my daughter. I speak to my husband differently than I speak to my father. I speak to all four of my siblings differently. Although I speak differently to each and every person, anyone who knows me knows my voice. Okay, I just said something!!! Did you catch what I was saying? In case you did not I will repeat. "Although I speak differently to each and every person, anyone who knows me knows my voice." God speaks to each of His children based upon the relationship that has been established. He speaks to us differently. God may very well speak to you through children, a preached word, your job, while driving, through visions, through teachers, pastors, friends, and family members. God may even speak to you through songs, during a spiritual conference, and even through individuals you don't necessarily like.

Let's look at another Scripture from the Bible that says, "For the word of God is living and active. Sharper than any double-edged sword, it penetrates even to dividing soul and spirit, joints and marrow; it judges the thoughts and attitudes of the heart." (*Hebrews 4:12*) The Word of the Lord is living and active. Translation: He is speaking. Here's another Scripture, which is actually a prayer of Paul that he prays in Philippians 1:9-10: "And this is my prayer: that your love may abound more and more in knowledge and depth of insight, so that you may be able to discern what is best and may be pure and blameless until the day of Christ...." We can pull out the following words: "knowledge – depth – insight – discernment. Knowledge is to know what God is speaking. When we see the word "depth," we can describe it as a deeply rooted and established in relationship with Christ. In concentrating on the word "insight," we know it is to discern and being able to see inside, which leads us to "discernment." We must know God. Grow deep in our relationship with Him. See what He is speaking and have a spirit of discernment to know His truth. That's powerful all by itself.

Got you! Remember, I'm always one step ahead of you and I am about to answer the very question you are thinking right now. "All Scripture is God-breathed and is useful for teaching, rebuking, correcting and training in righteousness." *(2 Timothy 3:16)* Did this Scripture answer your question? Good.

Yes, this chapter is going to be very short. God speaks through His Word: The Holy Bible — the written Scriptures. Throughout this book and the prayer workbook, I ask over and over again, "What is God speaking?" It is clear in Jeremiah 1:12 what God says. "...For I am watching to see that my Word is fulfilled." If He is watching to see that His Word is fulfilled, He's speaking.

STEPS ON THE JOURNEY

What is God speaking to you?

_____

_____

_____

_____

_____

_____

_____

_____

_____

_____

_____

_____

_____

_____

_____

_____

_____

_____

_____

_____

_____

_____

"For This Cause, I Bow..."
Ephesians 3:14 (KJV)

As I have been working with Gail on *Ready to Pray*, God has allowed me to be tested and to really understand what prayer is to me. And oh, what a test! There are times when I have no words (and as I sit here writing today, it is one of those times). I just need to be silent in the midst of noise and prayerfully, tune in to God. My days are not typically quiet as three little girls are constantly at my side, but when I can find a moment, even in the midst of the noise, to just sometimes say, "Jesus, I need you.... now," I pray that He hears me and grants just a little bit of His peace. Although my grandfather was a pastor, I did not grow up in a praying household, so God has had to place people in my life to help me learn how to pray along the way. And I have found during those points of brokenness, that God does hear and He does provide that "angel" who will speak or confirm His Word at exactly the right time. Sometimes it's a dream, sometimes it's a song, and sometimes it is His still, soft voice that I hear within my own heart.

I wish that I was eloquent or could speak an elaborate prayer that would garner an "Amen" from those listening. However, I simply am not that person. I speak to God just as I would speak to a trusted friend. Sometimes with tears, sometimes with frustration, sometimes with disappointment, but always, behind it all, love and respect. What I find is that when I speak with my heart, I can lay it all out to Him, not holding anything back, but just being honest about where I am, how much I need Him, how much I love Him, and how most times, I just want to feel His presence. And sometimes, I actually do.

—Stephanie Bright-Mayberry
Editor for *Ready To Pray*

Your Journey of Prayer and Worship

My name is _____ and this is my journey.

_____

_____

_____

_____

_____

_____

_____

_____

_____

_____

_____

_____

_____

_____

_____

_____

_____

_____

STEPS ON THE JOURNEY

30-DAY JOURNAL

Day One:

_____

Day Two:

_____

_____

_____

_____

_____

_____

_____

_____

_____

_____

_____

_____

_____

_____

_____

_____

_____

_____

_____

_____

_____

_____

_____

_____

_____

_____

_____

_____

_____

_____

Day Three:

_____

_____

_____

_____

_____

_____

_____

_____

_____

_____

_____

_____

_____

_____

_____

_____

_____

_____

_____

_____

_____

_____

_____

_____

_____

_____

_____

_____

Day Four:

_____

_____

_____

_____

_____

_____

_____

_____

_____

_____

_____

_____

_____

_____

_____

_____

_____

_____

_____

_____

_____

_____

_____

_____

_____

_____

_____

_____

_____

_____

Day Five:

_____

_____

_____

_____

_____

_____

_____

_____

_____

_____

_____

_____

_____

_____

_____

_____

_____

_____

_____

_____

_____

_____

_____

_____

_____

_____

_____

_____

Day Six:

Day Seven:

_____

_____

_____

_____

_____

_____

_____

_____

_____

_____

_____

_____

_____

_____

_____

_____

_____

_____

_____

_____

_____

_____

_____

_____

_____

_____

Day Eight:

Day Nine:

_____

_____

_____

_____

_____

_____

_____

_____

_____

_____

_____

_____

_____

_____

_____

_____

_____

_____

_____

_____

_____

_____

_____

_____

_____

_____

_____

Day Ten:

Day Eleven:

_____

_____

_____

_____

_____

_____

_____

_____

_____

_____

_____

_____

_____

_____

_____

_____

_____

_____

_____

_____

_____

_____

_____

_____

_____

_____

_____

_____

Day Twelve:

_____

_____

_____

_____

_____

_____

_____

_____

_____

_____

_____

_____

_____

_____

_____

_____

_____

_____

_____

_____

_____

_____

_____

_____

_____

_____

_____

_____

_____

_____

_____

_____

Day Thirteen:

Day Fourteen:

_____

_____

_____

_____

_____

_____

_____

_____

_____

_____

_____

_____

_____

_____

_____

_____

_____

_____

_____

_____

_____

_____

_____

_____

_____

_____

_____

_____

_____

Day Fifteen:

Day Sixteen:

Day Seventeen:

_____

_____

_____

_____

_____

_____

_____

_____

_____

_____

_____

_____

_____

_____

_____

_____

_____

_____

_____

_____

_____

_____

_____

_____

_____

_____

_____

_____

_____

Day Eighteen:

Day Nineteen:

_____

_____

_____

_____

_____

_____

_____

_____

_____

_____

_____

_____

_____

_____

_____

_____

_____

_____

_____

_____

_____

_____

_____

_____

_____

Day Twenty:

Day Twenty-one:

_____

_____

_____

_____

_____

_____

_____

_____

_____

_____

_____

_____

_____

_____

_____

_____

_____

_____

_____

_____

_____

_____

_____

_____

_____

Day Twenty-two:

Day Twenty-three:

_____

_____

_____

_____

_____

_____

_____

_____

_____

_____

_____

_____

_____

_____

_____

_____

_____

_____

_____

_____

_____

_____

_____

_____

_____

Day Twenty-four:

_____

_____

_____

_____

_____

_____

_____

_____

_____

_____

_____

_____

_____

_____

_____

_____

_____

_____

_____

_____

_____

_____

_____

_____

_____

_____

_____

_____

_____

Day Twenty-five:

Day Twenty-six:

_____

_____

_____

_____

_____

_____

_____

_____

_____

_____

_____

_____

_____

_____

_____

_____

_____

_____

_____

_____

_____

_____

_____

_____

_____

_____

_____

Day Twenty-seven:

_____

_____

_____

_____

_____

_____

_____

_____

_____

_____

_____

_____

_____

_____

_____

_____

_____

_____

_____

_____

_____

_____

_____

_____

_____

_____

Day Twenty-eight:

_____

_____

_____

_____

_____

_____

_____

_____

_____

_____

_____

_____

_____

_____

_____

_____

_____

_____

_____

_____

_____

_____

_____

_____

_____

_____

_____

_____

Day Twenty-nine:

_____

_____

_____

_____

_____

_____

_____

_____

_____

_____

_____

_____

_____

_____

_____

_____

_____

_____

_____

_____

_____

_____

_____

_____

_____

Day Thirty:

And now, all glory to God, who is able to keep you from stumbling, and who will bring you into his glorious presence innocent of sin and with great joy. All glory to him, who alone is God our Savior, through Jesus Christ our Lord. Yes, glory, majesty, power, and authority belong to him, in the beginning, now, and forevermore. Amen. Jude 24,25 (NLT)

PRAYER RESOURCES

Suggested Books on prayer:

Ready to Pray by Pastor Gail Dudley
A Journey to Victorious Praying by Bill Thrasher
    (Moody Publishers)
Developing a Prayer-Care-Share Lifestyle
    (HOPE Ministries)
Fresh Wind, Fresh Fire by Jim Cymbala
Intercessory Prayer by Dutch Sheets
I Told the Mountain to Move by Patricia Raybon
    (SaltRiver)
Learning to Pray Through the Psalms by James W. Sire
    (InterVaristy Press)
The Power of a Praying Woman by Stormie Omartian
    (Harvest House Publishers)
Pray with Purpose, Live with Passion by Debbie Williams
    (Howard Books)
Prayer by Richard J. Foster (HarperCollins Publishers)
Prayer 101: Experiencing the Heart of God
    by Warren Wiersbe (Cook Communications)

Praying God's Word by Beth Moore
    (Broadman & Holman Publishers)
Praying with Women of the Bible by Nancy Kennedy
    (Zondervan)
Possessing the Gates of the Enemy by Cindy Jacobs
Prayer Shield by C. Peter Wagner
What Happens When Women Pray by Evelyn Christensen
    (Cook Communications)
Spurgeon on Prayer & Spiritual Warfare
    by Charles Spurgeon
Disciple's Prayer Life by T.W. Hunt & Catherine Walker
How to Hear from God by Joyce Meyer
Possessing the Gates of the Enemy by Cindy Jacobs
Prayers that Avail Much
    by Germaine Copeland World Ministries, Inc.
Beyond the Veil by Alice Smith
Intercessory Prayer by Dutch Sheets
Prayer Shield by C. Peter Wagner
Fasting by Jentezen Franklin
A Hunger for God by John Piper
Intimacy with the Almighty by Charles R. Swindoll

Suggested DVD Series on Prayer:

When God's People Pray by Jim Cymbala

Suggested Study Bibles:

The Power of a Praying Woman Bible (NIV)
    by Stormie Omartian (Harvest House Publishers)

Suggested Workshops:

The 5-Hour Journey of Prayer Instruction is a one day/5-hour journey of prayer instruction designed to equip individuals, groups, and churches that desire to go deeper in their prayer journey as well as to be effective and impactful during prayer gatherings. For details of future conferences, please visit the website: www. ReadytoPray.info

Ministry in Motion Ministries is available to bring this workshop to you, sowing 10 percent of the profit back to your ministry or church. The cost per person for the conference is $50.00 per person (non-refundable). The cost includes the 215-page workbook. The cost of lunch is not included. The host may choose to charge this separately to the participants.

Suggested Websites on Prayer:

http://www.teachmetopray.com/
(free 52-week online prayer school)
http://www.globaldayofprayer.com/
http://www.presidentialprayerteam.org/
http://www.prayinglife.org/
http://www.allaboutprayer.org/
http://www.ReadytoPray.info

Suggested Bible Studies on Prayer:

Boldly Asking by Aletha Hinthorn
(Beacon Hill Press of Kansas City)
Connecting with God from Stonecroft Ministries
Disciple's Prayer Life: Walking in Fellowship with God
by T.W. Hunt & Catherine Walker
(LifeWay Church Resources)
Prayer: An Adventure with God by David Healey
(InterVarsity)

STATEMENT OF FAITH

GOD

We believe in one God, existing as three persons; Father, Son, and Holy Spirit, is the loving Creator of all that is, eternal and good, knowing all things, having all power, and desiring and inviting covenant relationship with humanity *(Matt. 28:19; 1 Tim. 1:17; Heb. 1:1-3; 9:14)*.

JESUS CHRIST

We believe in our Lord Jesus Christ, God manifest in the flesh. He alone is the Savior and Lord, the Son of God and God the Son, born of a virgin, the perfect example of humanity, crucified for the sin of the world, raised on the third day and who lives forever to make intercession for us. We confess the absolute lordship and leadership of the risen Jesus Christ, who is the Son of God and God the Son, and our soon-returning King *(Col. 1:15-20; Col. 2:9; John 1:1; Gal. 4:4; Phil. 3:10)*.

THE HOLY SPIRIT

We believe in God the Holy Spirit. At the point of salvation a person receives the Holy Spirit. We receive the abiding presence, peace, and power of the Holy Spirit in every believer as sufficient and necessary for normal Christian living *(Acts 1:8; Eph. 2:22; Rom. 8:9-30).*

SCRIPTURE

We believe in the Holy Scripture as originally given by Christ, divinely inspired, and revealed by God, unchanging and infallible Word of God, correct doctrine, the complete truth, authority, and relevance of every promise, provision, God's story of love and redemption (John 1:1; 2 Pet. 1:19-21; 2 Tim. 2:15; 3:16).

SALVATION

We believe in the salvation of the lost and sinful people by grace alone, through faith alone, in Christ alone. We accept the grace of God through the finished work of Jesus on the cross as victory for eternal and abundant life, and we maintain spiritual sonship and citizenship in the present and future Kingdom of God *(Rom. 10:9-10; Eph. 2:8-9).*

UNITY of THE BODY OF CHRIST

We believe in the unity of the Body of Christ and in the Spirit. Unity comprised of, teaching, prayer, fellowship, breaking of bread, meeting ministry needs, praise and worship, people being saved *(Eph. 4:1-6; Acts 2:42-47).*

HUMANITY

We celebrate the sacredness and uniqueness of every person as wonderfully created in the image of God and according to God's sovereign will, called to lives of Christlikeness through personal holiness, honor, and humility *(Heb. 2:6-12).*

SIN and EVIL

We acknowledge our sin and brokenness but refute anything that seeks to deny, discourage, or destroy the life that Jesus offers to all believers *(2 Cor. 4:1-18).*

MINISTRY

We believe that we should go, preach, and make disciples of Jesus Christ. We believe that we should be a witness for the Lord. We value the fellowship of Christian believers in loving community, gifted service, mutual encouragement and with godly leadership as representative of the presence of Christ on earth to meet the real needs of people *(Matt. 28:19-20; Acts 1:8; Acts 2:41-47).*

WORSHIP

We affirm that every person is called to glorify the living God completely, freely, and passionately by giving their lives in authentic relationship, their resources in responsible stewardship, and their devotion in faithful discipleship *(Jn. 4:23-24).*

PRAYER

We believe in communication with God and availability to God to do God's will in the earth. We believe that we must go to God with our heart and come away with His *(Matt.6).*

ABOUT THE AUTHOR

Gail E. Dudley

"...bringing you closer to Christ."

With a commitment to delivering messages that are both scriptural and applicable to real life situations, Gail E. Dudley shares the words that are spoken into her heart by the Holy Spirit and delivers those messages to the listener's ear.

One of her most rewarding experiences was participating as a conference speaker in Bulawayo, Zimbabwe, Africa, for The Women Unlimited of Word of Life International Annual Conference. Gail serves as a speaker and author with a passion to provide guidance to God's people as they navigate through their spiritual journey.

Currently Gail serves as a pastor at The Church at North Pointe, providing guidance, teaching discipleship studies, and overseeing multiple outreach efforts. She is also the Vice President of Diversity for Stonecroft Ministries, and works actively with the Mission America Coalition.

Gail is the wife of Reverend Dr. Kevin Dudley, senior pastor of The Church at North Pointe (Columbus, Ohio) and the loving mother of Alexander and Dominiq. Gail connects with people where they are in their journey and, upon hearing her speak, it is evident that Gail walks closely with the Lord, spends time daily in the Word, and seeks always to be ready to share God's truth for transforming lives.

BOOKING INFORMATION

If you would like to schedule Gail to speak at your retreat, your book club, or to do a book signing or a reading, please contact, Gail at:

www.GailDudley.com
GED@MIMToday.org
614-441-8178

We would love to hear from you. Send us your testimony and/or prayer request.

OTHER BOOKS BY GAIL

Ready to Change My Name ~
A Spiritual Journey from Fear to Faith

Ready to Pray Workbook ~
A Spiritual Journey of Praise and Worship

Ready to Pray (30 Minute Prayer CD)

Transparent Moments of Gail Dudley

Who Told You That? ~
The Truth Behind the Lies

ORDER ADDITIONAL COPIES TODAY

Gail E. Dudley
5550 Cleveland Avenue
Columbus, Ohio 43231-4049

Name: _____

Address: _____

City: _____ State: _____ Zip: _____

E-mail: _____

Would you like to join our mailing list? ❑ Yes   ❑ No thank you.

Telephone: (____) _____ - _____

Ready to Change My Name	qty: _____	($15.00 each + $2.50 S & H)
Ready to Pray (the Book)	qty: _____	($15.00 each + $2.50 S & H)
Ready to Pray (215 page Workbook)	qty: _____	($24.95 each + $3.50 S & H)
Ready to Pray (30 Minute Prayer CD)	qty: _____	($7.00 each + $2.50 S & H)
Who Told You That?	qty:_____	($17.50 each + $3.00 S & H)
Transparent Moments	qty: _____	($7.00 each + $3.00 S & H)

Book Total: $ _____   S & H Total: _____ = Grand Total $_____

Number of books being shipped: _____

Please make checks payable to:
Gail E. Dudley

Send payment to:
5550 Cleveland Avenue, Columbus, Ohio 43231-4049

Please allow two (2) weeks for shipping

CPSIA information can be obtained at www.ICGtesting.com
Printed in the USA
LVOW091906150212

268743LV00003B/6/P